Removing Blame from Eminent Scholars

Ibn Taymiyah
(1263 C.E -1328 C.E)

Alreshah.net

Canada

Copyright © 2018-20 by **Alreshah**

All rights reserved. No part of this publication may be reproduced, distributed, or transmitted in any form or by any means, without prior written permission.

Alreshah
www.Alreshah.net

If any error is found, please contact us through our website alreshah.net.

Book Layout © 2017 BookDesignTemplates.com

Removing Blame from Eminent Scholars/ Ibn Taymiyah. -- 1st ed.
ISBN 978-1-989875-06-3

Contents

Introduction 4
The First Reason 6
The Second Reason 15
The Third Reason 17
The Fourth Reason 21
The Fifth Reason 23
The Sixth Reason 25
The Seventh Reason 29
The Eighth Reason 31
The Ninth Reason 33
The Tenth Reason 36
The End 83

• CHAPTER 1 •

Introduction

In the name of Allah, the Most Merciful the Most Gracious

Praise is due to Allah for His signs. I bear witness that there is no deity except Allah, alone, without a partner in His earth and His heaven, and I bear witness that Muhammad is His servant, Messenger and the final of his Prophets; may Allah bestow upon him, all of them, his family and his companions a lasting blessing and peace until the day of meeting Him.

Now then; the Muslims must – after alliance with Allah and His Messenger (PBUH) – ally themselves with the believers, as stipulated by the Holy Qur'an, particularly with scholars, who are the successors of Prophets, whom Allah made like stars sought for guidance in the darkness of the land and sea. The Muslims unanimously affirm their uprightness and knowledge, for every nation before the advent of Muhammad (PBUH) deem their scholars the most wretched among them, except the Muslims, who deem their scholars the finest among them. They are the successors of the Messenger (PBUH) in his Ummah and the revivers of what has died of his Sunnah. With them, the Book was established, and with it they were established. The Book spoke through them, and they spoke with it.

It should be known that there is none of the scholars – who are widely accepted by the Ummah – who deliberately contradicts the Messenger (PBUH) in anything of his sunnah, whether small or large. They are in an affirmative agreement about the compulsoriness of following the Messenger (PBUH) and that the words of every human being are subject to acceptance and rejection except the Messenger (PBUH). However, if a view of any of them is found to contradict an authentic hadith, he must have an excuse for disregarding such hadith.

Excuses are restricted to three types:
The first: Not believing that the Prophet (PBUH) said it.
The second: Not believing that this saying concerns the issue at hand.
The third: Believing that provision to be abrogated.
These three types branch into various reasons.

IBN TAYMIYAH

• CHAPTER 2 •

The First Reason

The hadith did not reach him. Whoever did not hear of the hadith is not obligated to be aware of its entailment. If the hadith did not reach him – and he spoke about that issue according to the predominant meaning of a verse or another hadith, according to Qiyas (Deductive Analogy) or according to Istis'hab (Presumption of Continuity) – his view may agree with the hadith sometimes and disagree sometimes.

That reason is the prevalent in most of the early scholar's views that contradict some hadiths.

For complete knowledge of all the Messenger's (PBUH) hadiths is not granted to any one of the Ummah.

Sometimes, the Prophet (PBUH) spoke, delivered fatwa, ruled or acted, and he was heard or seen by those who were present, who – or some of whom – conveyed it to others, so knowledge of that incident reached whomever Allah wills of scholars from the Companions, Followers and those who came after them. Then in another instance, he spoke, delivered fatwa, ruled or acted, and was witnessed by some who were absent in the former situation and conveyed it to those they could, so the latters would have knowledge that the formers did not, and the formers would have knowledge that the latters did not. Scholars from the Companions and those after them are distinguished by the quantity or quality of their knowledge. As for someone encompassing all the Messenger's (PBUH) hadiths in knowledge is something that can never be claimed.

Consider, as an example for this, the Rightly-Guided Caliphs who are the most knowledgeable of the affairs, the sunnah and the life of the Messenger (PBUH), particularly Al-Siddiq[1] (may Allah be pleased with him) who did not part with him in accommodation or travel, but was with him most of the time, so much so that he even spent evenings with him conversing about the matters of the Muslims, and so was Umar ibn Al-Khattab, for he (PBUH) used to frequently say, "Abu Bakr, Umar and I entered …" "Abu Bakr, Umar and I came out …" "Abu Bakr, Umar and I went …" or, "Abu Bakr, Umar and I returned …" However, when Abu Bakr (may Allah be pleased with him) was asked about the grandmother's share of inheritance, he said,

---

[1] Abu Baker RA Title

"You [the inquiring grandmother] have nothing in the Book of Allah, and I do not know that you have anything in the sunnah of the Messenger of Allah (PBUH). Go away therefore, until I have asked the people." He asked them and Al-Mughirah ibn Shu'bah and Muhammad ibn Maslamah (may Allah be pleased with them) got up and testified that the Prophet (PBUH) gave a grandmother a sixth of the inheritance. This sunnah had also reached Imran ibn Hussain, and none of these three is like Abu Bakr (may Allah be pleased with him) or other caliphs, but they had exclusive knowledge of this sunnah, which the Ummah unanimously agreed to uphold.

Similarly, Umar ibn Al-Khattab (may Allah be pleased with him) did not know the sunnah of asking permission until Abu Moussa Al-Ash'ary (may Allah be pleased with him) told him of it and brought the Ansar as witnesses, although Umar (may Allah be pleased with him) is more knowledgeable than those who conveyed this sunnah to him.

Umar was also not aware that the woman inherits her husband's blood money, but believed that the blood money belongs to the male relatives, until Al-Dahhak ibn Sufian Al-Kilably – who was appointed by the Messenger (PBUH) in charge of some desert region – wrote to him telling him that the Messenger (PBUH) gave the wife of Ashyam Al-Dhababy a share of inheritance from her husband's blood money. Therefore, he renounced his view and said, "If we hadn't heard that, we would have ruled differently."

He also did not know the provision of Magians in Jizyah until Abd Al-Rahman ibn Awf told him that the Messenger (PBUH) said, "Follow the same sunnah with them that you follow with the people of the Book."

When he arrived at Sargh and heard that the black plague had spread in the Levant, he sought the council of the early Migrants who were with him, then the Ansar, then those who embraced Islam after the Conquest [of Mecca], and each of them expressed his opinion, but none of them told him of a sunnah, until Abd Al-Rahman ibn Awf came and told him of the Messenger's (PBUH) sunnah concerning the plague and that he said, "If it breaks out in a land where you are present, do not go out escaping from it, and if you hear that it has broken out in a land, do not go to it."

He and Ibn Abbas discussed the matter of the man who has doubts inside his prayer [e.g. doubting how many rak'ahs he has performed], and he did not know the sunnah regarding that at that time, until Abd Al-Rahman ibn Awf narrated that the Prophet (PBUH) said, "He should cast aside his doubt and base his prayer on what he is sure of."

He was travelling one a time and wind was stirred, so he said, "Who would narrate to us about wind?" Abu Hurairah said [narrating this story], "What he said reached me while I was in the back of the convoy, so I prodded my riding animal until I caught up with him, and I reported to him what the Prophet (PBUH) commanded upon the blowing of the wind."

These are matters that he had not known until he was informed of it by those who are not as knowledgeable as he was. There are other matters the sunnah concerning which did not reach him, so he ruled or delivered fatwa therein differently, just as he ruled in the blood money of fingers that it is different according to the finger's use, when Abu Moussa and ibn Abbas – who are inferior to him in knowledge – had knowledge that the Prophet (PBUH) said, "This one and that one are equal" – referring to the thumb and pinky. When news of this sunnah reached Mu'awiyah in his governorship, he ruled according to it, and the Muslims had no choice but to follow it. This was not a slander to Umar, for he did not know of the hadith.

Similarly, he used to forbid the person in the state of Ihram to put on perfume before Ihram and before departing to Mecca after the stoning of Aqabah, as did his son Abdullah (may Allah be pleased with them) and other people of merit who did not hear the hadith narrated by Aishah (may Allah be pleased with her) that she perfumed the Messenger (PBUH) before he performed Ihram and when he ended it before performing Tawaf around the [Holy] House.

He also used to command the wearer of leather socks to wipe [water] over it until he took it off with no regard to duration, and he was followed in that regard by a group of early Muslims. The hadiths concerning duration, which were known to be authentic by some who were not equal to them in knowledge, had not reached them. This was narrated from the Prophet (PBUH) in various authentic narrations.

Similarly, Uthman ibn Affan had no knowledge that the widowed woman spends the waiting term in the house where he died, until Al-Furay'ah bint Malik – the sister of Abu Saied Al-Khudry – narrated to him her story, when her husband died and the Prophet (PBUH) said to her, "Stay in your house until the prescribed term is fulfilled." Thereupon, Uthman upheld it.

He was presented once with game that was hunted for him, and he was about to eat it, until Ali (may Allah be pleased with him) told him that the Prophet (PBUH) has once returned meat that was presented to him.

Similarly, Ali (may Allah be pleased with him) said, "Whenever I heard a hadith from the Messenger (PBUH), Allah benefitted me as much as He willed with it, and whenever someone else narrated [a hadith] to me, I asked him to swear to it, and if he did, I believed him. Abu Bakr narrated to me, and truthful is Abu Bakr, …" before mentioning the well-known hadith of the Repentance Prayer.

He, as well as Ibn Abbas and others, stated as fatwa that if the widowed woman was pregnant, her waiting term is the longest of the two terms, and they had not heard the Messenger's ruling for Subay'ah Al-Aslamiyyah, as the Prophet (PBUH) told her that her waiting term is until she gives birth.

He, as well as Zaid, ibn Umar and others, stated as fatwa that when the husband of Al-Mufawwadhah dies, she has no dowry, and they had not heard the Messenger's (PBUH) judgment in Barwa' bint Washiq.

This is a vast topic where what is reported about the Messenger's (PBUH) Companions is very large in number.

As for what is reported about others, it cannot be enumerated, for it amounts to thousands. These [the Companions] where the most knowledgeable, pious and righteous of the Ummah, and those who came after them are less perfect. Therefore, being unaware of some of the Sunnah is more appropriate for them and needs no clarification. Whoever believes that every authentic hadith has reached every Imam or a specific Imam is gravely and shamefully mistaken.

No one may say: "These hadiths were recorded and gathered, and so lack of knowledge about them is farfetched." For these renowned books in Sunnah were gathered after the widely-followed Imams were extinct. Nevertheless, it is not acceptable to claim that the Messenger's (PBUH) hadiths are confined to certain books.

Even if it was assumed that the hadith were confined to them, not everything in books is known to the scholar, and this is hardly ever possible for anyone. One may have many books without encompassing everything therein in knowledge. Rather those [scholars] who lived before these books were gathered were much more knowledgeable of the Sunnah than the latters, because many of what reached them and was deemed authentic by them may not have reached us except through unknown narrators or with disconnected chains of narration, or may not have reached us at all. Their books were their hearts which contained many-fold what is in the books. This is undoubted by anyone who is acquainted with the subject matter.

No one may say: "Whoever is not aware of all hadiths cannot be a Mujtahid." Because if it was a prerequisite for the Mujtahid to be aware of everything the Prophet (PBUH) said and did concerning provisions, then there is no Mujtahid in the Ummah. Rather it is the capacity of the scholar to be aware of the majority of that and most of it so that nothing is unknown to him except few of details, then he may contradict the few of details that did not reach him and be excused therefore.

• CHAPTER 3 •

The Second Reason

The hadith did reach him but it was not deemed authentic by him, either because his narrator, his narrator's narrator or anyone in the chain of narrators was regarded by him as unknown, untrustworthy or unreliable in memorization, or because it reached him with a discontinuous – rather than a continuous – chain of narrators, or because the wording of the hadith was not verified, although that same hadith was narrated by trustworthy narrators to others with a continuous chain of narrators. This is possible if the others knew whoever was unknown to him to be trustworthy, or if it were narrated by other narrators than those he deemed untrustworthy, or if it were continuous from a path other than the discontinuous one, or if its wording was verified by memorizing hadith scholars, or if that narration had enough proofs and follow-ups to clarify its authenticity.

This is also very common, and it is more common among the Followers and their followers until the renowned Imams after them than it is in the first era and the first part. For hadiths had grown widespread and well-known, but they reached many scholars through weak paths of narration, despite reaching others through other authentic paths. Thus, they became solid evidence from those paths although they did not reach whoever contradicted them from the same paths. That is why, it was found in the words of multiple Imams to suspend the upholding of the hadith pending its authenticity, by saying, "My view in this matter is such and such, but a hadith was narrated in this regard saying so and so, and if it was found authentic, then it is my view.".

CHAPTER 4

The Third Reason

Belief in the weakness of the hadith through Ijtihad that someone else contradicted, while disregarding other paths, whether he was right, the contradictor was right or both of them were right – according to those who say: every Mujtahid is right. There are reasons for that, including:

- One of them believes the narrator to be weak and the other believes him to be trustworthy. The study of narrators is a vast field. The one who believes in his weakness may be the right one because of his knowledge of a disqualifying factor, while the other one may be the right one for his knowledge that that factor is not disqualifying, either because it is not disqualifying in principle or because the narrator had an excuse that prevents it from taking effect. This is a vast topic. Scholars specialized in narrators and their affairs have of agreement and disagreement in that regard as other scholars have in their respective fields.

- He does not believe that the narrator heard the hadith from the person from whom he is narrating, while the other one believes he heard from him, for well-known reasons that necessitate that.

- The narrator had two states [in his life]: a state of uprightness and a state of turbulence, such as growing senile or his books burning. Thus, whatever he narrated in the state of uprightness is authentic, and whatever he narrated in the state of turbulence is weak. The scholar may not know in which state that hadith was, while others know it was narrated in the state of uprightness.

- The narrator may have forgotten that hadith and did not remember it later or denied narrating it, and the scholar believes this is an ailment that necessitates disregarding the hadith, while others think it is a solid evidence. The issue is well-known.

- Many of the Hijaz scholars believe that a hadith narrated by an Iraqi or a Levantine narrator is not solid evidence if it did not have an origin in Hijaz, so much so that one of them said, "Regard the hadiths of the people of Iraq as you would regard the hadiths of the People of the Book. Neither believe nor disbelieve them." Another one was asked, "Sufian, from Mansour, from Ibrahim, from Alqamah, from Abdullah: is [a hadith narrated through that path of narration] a solid evidence?" He said, "If it did not have an origin in Hijaz, then no." This is due to their belief that the people of Hijaz verified the Sunnah and had no oddities therein, while the hadiths of the Iraqis had turbulence that necessitated disregarding them. Some Iraqis think that the hadiths of Levantines are not solid evidence. However, most scholars do not regard that as a weakening factor. Whenever the chain of narrators is good, the hadith is a solid evidence, whether it was from Hijaz, the Levant, Iraq or elsewhere.

Abu Dawud Al-Sijistany wrote a book about the geographically-unique hadiths, clarifying the hadiths exclusive to every place that are not found with continuous chains of narrators elsewhere, including Madinah, Mecca, Taif, Damascus, Homos, Kufa, Basra and so on. There are many other reasons.

CHAPTER 5

The Fourth Reason

Having conditions for the acceptance of the hadith narrated by an individual, upright and reliable narrator while others contradict [these conditions], such as some of them stipulating examining the hadith against the Book and the Sunnah, some of them stipulating that the narrator must be a jurist if the hadith contradicted the Qiyas of foundations, and some of them requiring the wide-spreading and prevalence of the hadith if it concerned a universal affliction, as well as other conditions known in their respective fields.

• CHAPTER 6 •

The Fifth Reason

The hadith reached him and was deemed authentic by him but he forgot it. This happens with the Qur'an and the Sunnah, such as the famous story where Umar (may Allah be pleased with him) was asked about a man who became Junub[2] in travel and could not find water, so he said,

This is a sunnah that Umar witnessed then forgot, so much so that he delivered a fatwa contradicting it, so Ammar reminded him but he did not remember, and he did not accuse Ammar of lying, rather he commanded him to narrate it.

A stronger example is that he was giving a sermon and said, "Anyone who gives a dowry that exceeds the dowry of the Prophet's (PBUH) wives and daughters, I will force him to reduce it to that amount." Thereupon, a woman said, "O Amir

---

[2] Junub is person ritually impure due to sexual intercourse or seminal discharge

Al-Mu'minin! Why do you deny us something that Allah has granted us?" Then she recited, "you have given one of them a great amount [in gifts]" [4:20]. Thereupon, Umar upheld her view. He had known the verse but he forgot it.

Moreover, what is narrated that Ali reminded Al-Zubair on the Battle of the Camel of something that the Messenger (PBUH) had entrusted to the two of them, and he kept reminding him until he left the battle.

This is frequent with the formers and the latters.

CHAPTER 7

The Sixth Reason

Lack of knowledge of the denotation of the hadith, sometimes due to the word stated in the hadith being unfamiliar to him, such as the words: Al-Muzabanah, Al-Muhaqalah, Al-Mukhabarah, Al-Mulamasah, Al-Munabadhah, Al-Gharar as well as other strange words which the scholars may disagree in interpreting them.

Also, such as the hadith attributed to the Prophet (PBUH) that he said, "There is no divorce and no manumission at the time of coercion" for they interpreted the word 'Ghalaq' as coercion, but those who disagree with that do not uphold that interpretation.

Sometimes, it is because the meaning of the word in his dialect and usage is different than its meaning in the Prophet's (PBUH) dialect, and he interpreted it according to what he understood in his dialect based on the fact that the language's endurance is the natural assumption. For example, some of them heard narrations about permitting 'Nabidh' and thought it is a type of intoxicant, because it is their dialect, but it means [date fruits] set aside to sweeten the water before they become fermented, for it was explained in many authentic hadiths. When they heard the term 'Khamr' in the Qur'an and the Sunnah, they believed it exclusively meant the fermented raw grape juice, because this is what it means in the language, although many authentic hadiths clarified that 'Khamr' means every intoxicating drink.

Sometimes, it is because the term is polysemous, abridged or oscillating between literality and figurativeness, so he interprets it according to what is more likely correct in his perspective, even if the other meaning was the intended one, just as a group of the Companions in the beginning interpreted the white thread [the light of dawn] and the black thread [the darkness of the night] as literal threads.

And just as others interpreted the verse, "and wipe over your faces and your hands" [4:43] and [5:6], to mean the hand until the armpit.

Sometimes, it is because the meaning of the text is ambiguous, for the denotations of words are very vast, and people vary in perceiving them and understanding the meanings of words are according to the grants and endowments given to them by the Truth (the Almighty). One may know the denotations in general but does not realize that this meaning falls under that general understanding, or he might realize it once and then forget it later. This is a very vast topic which only Allah can encompass. Sometimes, one might err and interpret words in a way that is not possible within the realm of the Arabic language with which the Messenger (PBUH) was sent.

CHAPTER 8

The Seventh Reason

Belief that there are no denotations in the hadith. The difference between this one and the previous one is that the former did not know the denotation while the latter knew the denotation but believed it is not a correct denotation, by having foundations that confute such denotation, whether it was, in the same matter, correct or wrong. For example, Believing that:

- the specific general [statement] is not evidence,
- the understood meaning is not ground for reasoning,
- the general associated with a reason is confined to that reason,

- the abstract command does not necessitate obligation or immediateness,

- the name defined with 'ال' cannot be generalized,

- negating the verbs does not negate its essence or all its provisions,

- or that the evidence is not universal, so universality cannot be claimed in denotations and meanings.

And so on of what is too many to enumerate. Because for half of the Islamic Jurisprudence Principles, the debated issues fall under this category. Although the abstract foundations did not encompass all the debated denotations and individual denotation genres go into it, are they of this genre or not? For example, believing that this specific term is abridged, to be polysemous without any sign to specify the intended meaning, and so on.

CHAPTER 9

The Eighth Reason

Believing that this denotation was confuted by something that indicated it is not the intended denotation, such as confuting the general [statement] with a specific one, the absolute with a restricted one, the abstract command with what negates obligation, or the literal with what indicates figurativeness, and so on of the types of confutation. This is also a vast topic, for the contradiction of words' denotations and favoring some of them to others is a large sea.

• CHAPTER 10 •

The Ninth Reason

Believing that the hadith is opposed by what indicates its weakness or abrogation, or interpreting it – if it was interpretable – with what is unanimously accepted to be fit for opposition, such as a verse, another hadith or scholarly consensus. This is divided into two categories:

First: believing that the opposing element is superior in general, and one of the three cases is determined without specifying which one. Sometimes, he specifies one of them, by believing it is abrogated or interpreted. In that case, he may err in abrogation and mix the former with the latter, or he may err in interpretation and interpret the hadith in a way that is not possible with such wording, or if something that refutes it exists. Even if the opposing element confutes it in general, it may not be sufficient evidence, and the opposing hadith may not be as strong as the original in the chain of narrators or in text. Here, the aforementioned reasons and others come in the former hadith, and the alleged consensus is mostly lack of knowledge of opposition.

We have found among the eminent scholars some who upheld views mainly because of their lack of knowledge of opposition, although the apparent evidence they had necessitate otherwise. However, the scholar cannot introduce a view the speaker of which is unknown to him while knowing that scholars have contradicted such view. Some of them even suspend their view by saying, "If there is a consensus in the matter, it is more worthy to be followed. Otherwise, my view is so and so."

This is like whoever says, "I did not know of anyone who permitted the slave's testimony," although its acceptance is reported from Ali, Anas, Shuraih and others.

Or whoever says, "The partially emancipated does not inherit," despite his inheritance being narrated from Ali and ibn Masoud, and there is a good hadith narrated from the Prophet (PBUH) in this regard.

Another one says, "I do not know of anyone who deemed the invocation of blessing upon the Prophet (PBUH) in the prayer obligatory," when deeming it obligatory is conveyed from Abu Jaafar Al-Baqir.

Removing Blame from Eminent Scholars

That is because the capacity of many scholars is to know the views of scholars with whom he was contemporaneous in his country – which is a great measure – and the views of other groups of scholars. For example, you find many of the early scholars only aware of the views of the scholars of Madinah and Kufa, and many of the latter scholars only aware of the views of two or three of the widely-followed imams, and they regard whatever contradicts that to contradict the consensus, because he does not know who said it, and he keeps hearing its opposing views. Thus, such scholar cannot uphold a contradictory hadith that lest it contradicts consensus, or for believing it is so, as consensus is the greatest evidence. This is the excuse of many people in disregarding most of what they disregard. Some of them are truly excused therein, while others use it as an excuse without being truly excused. Such is true for many of the reasons before and after this.

• CHAPTER 11 •

The Tenth Reason

Confuting it with what indicates its weakness, abrogation or interpretation, which others do not regard confuting in principle or which is not truly a superior contradictor, such as many Kufis confuting the authentic hadith with the predominant denotation of the Qur'an, and believing that the predominant denotation of the Qur'an, which may indicate generality and so on, is given precedence over the certain denotation of the hadith. In this case, he may believe what is not predominant to be predominant, because of the various denotations of the statement. That is why they rejected the hadith of the single witness and the oath, although others know that there is nothing in the predominant denotation of the Qur'an to prohibit ruling based on a single witness and an oath, and even if there were, the Sunnah is the interpreter of the Qur'an from their perspective.

Removing Blame from Eminent Scholars

There are famous words for Al-Shafi'y (may Allah be merciful to him) concerning this rule, and for Ahmad (may Allah be merciful to him) there is the renowned message in refuting whoever claims that the Sunnah's interpretation is dispensable with the predominant meaning of the Qur'an, and he included of evidence therein what is too much to be stated here.

For example: Rejecting the hadith that specifies what is general in the Qur'an or restricts what is absolute therein or has an addition to it. Those who uphold that view believe that the addition to the text, such as restricting the absolute, abrogates [the Qur'anic text], and that specifying the general abrogates [the Qur'anic text].

Another example is that a group of the Madinah scholars confute the authentic hadith with the practice of the people of Madinah because their consensus is contradictory to the report and their consensus is a superior evidence to the report. For example, confuting the hadith about the council's choice based on that rule. However, most scholars may state that the Madinah scholars disagreed about this issue, and that if they were in consensus and others opposed them, the superior evidence would be the report.

Another the example is that a group of scholars from the two cities [i.e. Madinah and Kufa] confute some hadiths with express Qiyas, based on the rule that comprehensive foundations are not refuted with such a report, and so on of the types of contradiction, whether the contradictor is right or wrong.

These ten reasons are explicit, and in many hadiths, it is possible for the scholar to have an excuse for leaving them that we did not know, for the realms of knowledge are vast, and we are not aware of everything within the minds of scholars. The scholar may or may not express his argument, and if he did express it, it may or may not reach us, and if it did reach us, we may or may not realize his excuse, whether or not the excuse is correct in that instance. However, even if we allow this, we must not desist from a view evidenced by an authentic hadith and upheld by a group of scholars to another view stated by another scholar who may have evidence to refute the former evidence, even if he was more knowledgeable, for error is more likely to occur in the views of scholars than in the legal evidence. The legal evidence is Allah's argument against all His servants, unlike the scholar's view.

The legal evidence cannot be wrong unless confuted by another evidence, but the scholar's opinion is not like that. If upholding this allowance was permitted, we would not have any evidence left where such is permitted, but the intended message is that he [the scholar] himself is excused for disregarding such evidence, and we are excused for disregarding his disregard. Allah (the Almighty) said, "That was a nation which has passed on. It will have [the consequence of] what it earned, and you will have what you have earned. And you will not be asked about what they used to do." [2:134] He also said, "And if you disagree over anything, refer it to Allah and the Messenger" [4:59]. No one may confute a hadith of the Prophet (PBUH) with the saying of any person. Just like Ibn Abbas (may Allah be pleased with both of them) when a man asked him about a juristic problem, and when he responded to him with a hadith, the man said to him, "Abu Bakr and Umar said such and such." So, Ibn Abbas said, "Stones shall soon fall upon you from heaven. I say: "Allah's Messenger (PBUH) said so and so," and you say, "Abu Bakr and Umar said such and such?!""

Since disregard happens due to some of these reasons, so if there is an authentic hadith which includes allowance, forbiddance or a provision, one should not think that the aforementioned scholars who contradicted it would be punished for making lawful what is unlawful or vice versa or for not judging by what Allah has revealed. Similarly, if the hadith contained a threat for an act, such as curse, wrath or punishment, we cannot say that the scholar who permitted such act shall fall under that threat. We do not know amidst the Ummah of any dispute concerning that except something narrated from some of the Mu'tazila of Baghdad, such as Al-Marisy and his peers, that they claimed that the mistaken Mujtahid is punished for his mistake. This is because the materialization of the threat is contingent on his knowledge of the unlawfulness, or his capacity to know the unlawfulness. If someone grew up in the desert or was new to Islam and committed a forbidden deed without knowing its unlawfulness, he does not bear a sin and is not subject to a legal punishment, even if he did not have a legal evidence as basis for deeming it lawful. Thus, whoever did not know the forbidding hadith, and he based his allowance on legal evidence is more worthy of being excused, and is therefore praised and rewarded for his Ijtihad. Allah (the Exalted) said, "And [mention] David and Solomon, when they judged concerning the field - when the sheep of a people overran it [at night], and We were witness to their judgement. And We gave understanding of the case to Solomon, and to each [of them] We gave judgement and knowledge ..." [21:78-79]. Thus, He attributed understanding to Solomon exclusively, and he praised both of them for knowledge and judgment.

In the Sahihs, Amr ibn Al-Aas narrated that the Prophet (PBUH) said, "If a judge gives a verdict according to the best of his knowledge and his verdict is correct (i.e. agrees with Allah and His Apostle's verdict) he will receive a double reward, and if he gives a verdict according to the best of his knowledge and his verdict is wrong, (i.e. against that of Allah and His Apostle) even then he will get a reward" Therefore, he clarified that the

Mujtahid who is wrong gets a reward for his Ijtihad, and his mistake is forgiven, this is because attaining correctness in all verdicts is either impossible or impractical. Allah (the Almighty) said, "and has not placed upon you in the religion any difficulty" [22:78]. He (the Almighty) also said, "Allah intends for you ease and does not intend for you hardship" [2:185].

It is stated in the Sahihs that the Prophet (PBUH) said to his Companions in the year of the Battle of the Trench, "None should offer the Dusk Prayer but at Bani Quraizah" and the time of Dusk Prayer came while they were on their way, so some of them said, "We shall not pray except in Bani Quraizah," while others said, "This is not what he wanted us to do," and they prayed on the way. He (PBUH) did not criticize either group.

The first group clung to the generality of the command, and saw the image of the prayer lapsing as included in that general command. The others had evidence that necessitated excluding that image from the generality and that the intended meaning was to march to those people with haste. This is an issue subjected to a well-known debate by the jurists: Is Qiyas exclusive for the general statement? Nevertheless, those who prayed along the way were more correct.

Similarly, when Bilal sold two Sa's for one Sa', the Prophet (PBUH) ordered him to return it, and did not apply the ruling for the usurer of deeming him disobedient, cursing and reproaching him, due to his lack of knowledge of its unlawfulness.

Similarly, when Adyy ibn Hatim and a group of the Companions thought that His saying (the Almighty), "until the white thread of dawn becomes distinct to you from the black thread [of night]" [2:187] means white and black threads. Therefore, each of them had next to his pillow two ropes: a black and a white one, and he kept eating until he could distinguish them from one another. The Prophet (PBUH) said to Adyy, "Then your pillow is too wide. It means the whiteness of dawn and the blackness of the night" Thus, he pointed to his lack of understanding of the meaning of the words and he did not base on that action defamation for the person who breakfasted in Ramadhan, although it is among the greatest major sins. This is unlike those who told the man with the fractured head that he is obligated to have a bath in the cold weather, so he did and he died as a result. He (PBUH) said, "They killed him, may Allah kill them! Could they not ask when they did not know? The cure for ignorance is inquiry" For these people made a mistake without Ijtihad, for they were not of the people of knowledge.

Similarly, he did not impose upon Usama ibn Zaid a penalty, blood-money or expatiation when he killed the man who said, "There is no deity except Allah," in the Battle of Al-Hurqat, for he believed killing him was justified based on his declaration of Islam being false, although killing him was unlawful. The early Muslims and the majority of scholars upheld that, that what the people of transgression deemed lawful of the blood of the people of justice via a reasonable interpretation does not impose a penalty, blood-money or expatiation, even though killing and fighting the people of justice is forbidden.

That condition that we stated for the materialization of the threat does not need to be stated in every instance, for knowledge of it is firmly established in the hearts, like the promise [of reward] for deeds which is contingent on dedication of the deed to Allah and not becoming nullified through apostasy, that condition does not need to be stated in every hadith concerning reward either. Even when the condition for the materialization of the threat is fulfilled, the judgment may default because of a deterrent. The deterrents of the materialization of the threat are many:

They include: repentance, asking for forgiveness, the good deeds that erase sins, the adversity and calamities of the worldly life, the intercession of an obeyed intercessor and the mercy of the Most Merciful of the merciful. If all these are absent – and they will not all be absent except for someone who became insolent, rebelled and ran away from Allah like a camel runs away from its master – then the threat will befall him. This is because the reality of the threat is to clarify that this deed is the cause of this punishment, which indicates the unlawfulness and ugliness of that deed. As for believing that everyone who performed that cause must be subjected to that effect, this is certainly false, due to the contingency of that effect upon the presence of the condition and the absence of all deterrents.

To clarify that: Whoever disregards a hadith must fall under one of three categories:

- Either that disregard is permitted according to the consensus of the Muslims, such as disregard by someone whom the hadith did not reach and who was not remiss in pursuit while being in need for delivering fatwa or adjudicating, such as what we mentioned about the rightly-guided caliphs and others. No Muslim doubts that this one does not bear any dishonor for his disregard.

- Or it may be an unpermitted disregard, and this hardly ever comes from an imam, God willing.

- However, what is feared for some scholars is that the man may be incapable of reaching the provision of that issue, and he rules without having the means to do so, although he had consideration and Ijtihad in the matter. He may alternatively be remiss in deduction, so he reaches a conclusion without giving due consideration, despite clinging to an argument, or he may be dominated by a habit or a purpose that prevents him from giving due consideration in order to consider what contradicts what he has. Even if he did not speak without consideration and Ijtihad, the limit that the Ijtihad must reach may not be fulfilled for the Mujtahid.

That is why scholars feared such a situation, lest the proper Ijtihad was not met in that specific issue, for these are sins. However, the punishment of the sin reaches its committer if he does not repent, and it may be erased by invoking forgiveness, righteousness, adversity, intercession and mercy. Excluded from that is whoever is dominated and overcome by inclination so he supports what he knows to be false, or whoever states positively the rightness or wrongness of a statement without knowledge of the affirming and opposing denotations of that statement, for these two kinds of people are in Hellfire, as the Prophet (PBUH) said, "The judges are three: Two judges are in Hellfire, and a judge is in Paradise. The one in Paradise is a man who knew the truth and ruled according to it. As for the two who are in Hellfire, they are a man who ruled to the people ignorantly, and a man who knew the truth and ruled contrary to it" The same goes for the deliverers of fatwa.

However, the materialization of the threat for the specific person also has deterrents, just as we clarified. So, if assumed some of that was done by one of the eminent scholars praised by the Ummah – although this is farfetched or unrealistic – they will not lack one of these reasons, and even if it happened, this will not disparage their leadership at all, for we do not believe they are infallible; we rather know they are susceptible to sin, and we hope for them the highest ranks despite that, for what Allah privileged them of righteous deeds and adherence to the Sunnah in their lives and because they did not persist in committing a sin. They are not a higher rank than the Companions, for whom this also applies concerning their Ijtihad in the problems, issues and blood that was among them and so on.

In addition, with knowledge that the aforementioned disregarder is not only excused, but also rewarded, this does not prevent us from following the authentic hadiths for which we know no opposition, or believing in the compulsoriness of working in accordance to them and spreading them. This is undebated among scholars.

They are divided into:

- What is of a certain denotation: by having a certain chain of narrators and text, which means what we are certain that the Messenger (PBUH) said and certain of the meaning he intended from it.

- What is of a predominant, uncertain denotation.

As for the first type, its entailment must be believed, concerning both the knowledge and the deeds. This is undebated among scholars in general, but they may disagree about some reports: is it of a certain or an uncertain chain of narrators? Is it of a certain or an uncertain denotation? Such as their disagreement about the report of the individual that which the Ummah received with acceptance and belief or unanimously agreed to uphold. Most jurists and theologians believe it entails certainty, while others believed it does not.

Similarly, the report narrated through multiple paths of narration each affirming the other by specific people, may yield certain knowledge to one who is knowledgeable about these paths, the manners of these narrators, and other presumptions and addendums surrounding the report. However, certainty of that report will not occur to whoever does not share in that knowledge with him.

This is why the master, well-versed scholars of hadith may have complete certainty about some reports which other scholars do not think, let alone know, are authentic. This implies that the certainty-yielding report may yield it through the quantity of narrators sometimes, from the attributes of narrators sometimes, from the narration itself sometimes, from the narrator's comprehension of it sometimes, and from the narrated report sometimes. Sometimes, the report narrated by a few yields certainty because of their piety and reliability which remove doubts of lying or error, while many fold that number of other narrators does not yield certainty.

This is the unsuspected truth, and it is the view of the majority of jurists, hadith scholars and groups of theologians. Some groups of theologians and some jurists believe that every number of people whose report yields certainty of an issue, the report of the same number of people yield certainty in every issue. This is certainly false, but this is not the time to clarify that.

As for the effect of presumptions external to the narrators in certainty of the report, we did not mention it, for these presumptions may entail certainty if they were disentangled from the report, so if they themselves yield certainty, they are not made subsequent to the report, and the report is not made subsequent to them either. Rather, each of them is a path to certainty sometimes and to uncertainty sometimes, even if it coincided that both of them entailed certainty, or one entails certainty while the other entailed uncertainty, for whoever is more knowledgeable of reports may be certain in the authenticity of reports that others, who are less knowledgeable, do not.

Sometimes they debate whether it is of certain denotation due to their disagreement whether that hadith it is monosemous or polysemous and, if it were polysemous, whether it contains what confutes the inferior denotation. This is also a vast topic. Some scholars may be certain of the denotations of hadiths that others are not, either because of their knowledge that the hadith can only produce this denotation, their knowledge that the hadith cannot be interpreted in the other denotation, or other evidence that yields certainty.

As for the second type, the one of predominant denotation, this must be upheld in legal provisions according to the consensus of regarded scholars. If it includes a provision of certainty, such as a threat and so on, they debated it. Groups of jurists believe that if the report of an upright individual narrator that includes threat for a deed, it must be upheld to make unlawful that deed, but the threat is not upheld unless it is certain, and so is the case if the text was certain but the denotation was not. This is how they interpreted the saying of Aishah (may Allah be pleased with her), "Tell Zaid that he has invalidated his Jihad with the Messenger (PBUH) unless he repents."

They said: Aishah (may Allah be pleased with her) mentioned the threat because she was aware of it. We use her report as evidence for unlawfulness, but we do not uphold that threat, because the hadith was narrated to us through an individual report.

Their argument is that a threat is a matter of certainty, so it is not proven except by that which yields certainty. In addition, if the committer of the deed believed in its lawfulness through his Ijtihad, the threat does not apply to him. According to these scholars, the hadiths of threats are ground for deeming the deeds unlawful in general, but the threat is not confirmed unless the denotation is certain.

Similarly, the majority of scholars' use of the recitations that are authentically narrated from some scholars, despite not being in Uthman's Mus'haf, as evidence, for they include knowledge and deeds, and they are authentic individual reports. They used them as evidence for the deeds without confirming them as Qur'an, for it is one of the matters of certainty, which are only confirmed with certainty.

Most jurists believe, and this is the view of the majority of the early scholars, that these hadiths are evidence in everything they included, of the unlawfulness of the deed and the threat. For the Messenger's (PBUH) Companions kept confirming, with these hadiths, the threat as they confirmed the unlawfulness of the deed, and express the applicability of the threat therein to the committer of the deed in general. This is widely known from them in their speeches and fatwas. That is because the threat is among the legal provisions that are proven by the predominant evidence sometimes and the certain evidence sometimes. What is required is not full certainty of the threat, but rather belief that includes both certainty and predominant supposition. This is also what is required for provisions of certainty.

There is no difference between one's belief that Allah forbid that deed and threatened its committer with punishment in general, or belief that Allah forbid it and promised its committer with a certain punishment, for both of them are reports from Allah, and just as it is permitted to report from Him in the first instance by the sheer evidence, so is the case in the second instance. If someone even said, "Using it as ground to confirm the threat is more appropriate," he would be correct.

That is why they used to be more lenient in the chains of narrators of the hadith of enticement and intimidation than they were in the hadiths of provisions, for belief in the threat drives the souls to abandon the deed. If the threat is true, then one is saved, and if it is not true, and the true punishment is less than that, one who abandons such deed is not harmed by his belief in the graver punishment, because if he believed in the lighter punishment he may also be mistaken, and even if he did not believe in that graver punishment affirmatively or negatively, he may also be mistaken. That mistake may make the deed easier for him, causing him to commit it and deserve the graver punishment if it is true, or fulfil the reason for deserving it. For error in the belief in both assumptions: assumption of the threat's existence and assumptions of its nonexistence, are alike, and deliverance from punishment through the assumption of the threat's existence is more likely. Therefore, that assumption is more appropriate.

With that evidence, most scholars gave preference to the forbidding evidence over the permitting evidence, and many jurists followed the path of caution in many provisions based on that. As for caution in the deed, it is unanimously approved by the wise in general. If his fear of error by believing in the threat faced by his fear of error by unbelieving in it, the evidence entailing believing in it and the deliverance resulting from believing remain as two unchallenged pieces of evidence.

No one may say: "The lack of certain evidence for the threat is a proof of its nonexistence, just like the lack of recurrent narration for the recitations exceeding what is in the Mus'haf." For the lack of evidence is not proof of the opposite, and whoever confuted something of the topics of certainty because of the lack of certain evidence for its existence – as is the manner of a group of theologians – is clearly mistaken. However, if we know that the existence of something necessitates the existence of evidence, and we learned the lack of evidence, we are certain in the nonexistence of that necessitating thing, because the lack of the necessitated is evidence for the lack of the necessitating. We learned that there is an abundance of reasons to convey the Book of Allah (the Exalted, the Majestic) and His religion, and that the Ummah must not conceal what needs to be conveyed generally, and since no sixth prayer or no other Surah were conveyed generally, we know for certain their nonexistence.

The topic of threats does not fall under that, for it is not necessary for every threat to be conveyed concurrently, just as it is not necessary for the legality of that deed. Therefore, it is proven that the hadiths containing threats must be upheld by believing that the committer of that deed is threatened with that threat, but the applicability of the threat to him is contingent on some conditions and has some deterrents.

This rule is explained through examples:

Including: that it is authentically narrated that the Prophet (PBUH) said, "Allah has cursed the accepter of usury, its payer, its two witnesses and the one who records it" It was also authentically narrated that he said to someone who sold two Sa's for a Sa' on the spot, "Woe! It is definite usury" He also said, "[Exchanging] wheat for wheat is usury unless it is done on the spot" as the hadith goes, which necessitates the admittance of the two types of usury, the excess usury and the delay usury in the [first] hadith. Then, there are those who heard his (PBUH) saying, "There is no usury (in money exchange) except when it is not done from hand to hand (i.e. when there is delay in payment)." So, they deemed exchanging two Sa's for a Sa' on the spot as lawful, such as Ibn Abbas (may Allah be pleased with both of them) and his companions, like Abu Al-Sha'thaa', Ataa', Tawus, Saied ibn Jubair, Ikrimah and other eminent scholars of Mecca, who are among the elites of the Ummah in knowledge and righteousness. No Muslim may believe that any of them in particular – or whoever imitated them as they should – will be reached by the usurer's curse, because they did that through a generally reasonable interpretation. It is said that Ibn Abbas and some of his companions renounced that, while others did not and did not know the [forbidding] text, so they are excused.

Similarly, what is reported about some of the virtuous of Madinah of having intercourse through the anus despite what Abu Dawud narrated that the Prophet (PBUH) said, "Whoever has intercourse with a woman in her anus, he has disbelieved in what was revealed to Muhammad" So, can a Muslim say that Such-and-such and So-and-so have disbelieved in what was revealed to Muhammad?

It was also authentically conveyed that he (PBUH) cursed ten related to Khamr: the one who presses it, the one who has it pressed, its drinker, as the hadith goes.

It was also authentically conveyed through various paths that he (PBUH) said, "Every drink that causes intoxication is Khamr" and said, "Every intoxicant is Khamr"

Umar (may Allah be pleased with him) spoke on the Messenger's (PBUH) pulpit and said between the Migrants and Al-Ansar, "Khamr is what stupefies the mind." Allah revealed the forbidding of Khamr, and it was revealed because of what they used to drink in Madinah. They had no drink except Fadhikh , and they had nothing of the wine of grapes. There were men among the best of the Ummah in knowledge and righteousness of the people of Kufa who believed that there is no Khamr except from grapes, and that the wine of everything apart from grapes and dates is not forbidden except the amount that intoxicates, and they used to drink the amount they thought was lawful. It is not permitted to say that they are subject to that threat, because of the excuse they had and their interpretation, or due to other deterrents. It is also not permitted to say that the drink they drank is not of the Khamr, the drinker of which is cursed, because the cause of the general saying must be included therein, and there was no grape wine in Madinah.

Moreover, the Prophet (PBUH) cursed the seller of Khamr, and some Companions (may Allah be pleased with them) sold wine, until news of it reached Umar, so he said, "May Allah curse So-and-so! Didn't he know that the Messenger (PBUH) said, "May Allah curse the Jews, because Allah made fat illegal for them but they sold it and ate its price'" He [the person who sold it] did not know that selling it is forbidden, and his lack of knowledge did not prevent Umar from clarifying the punishment of that sin, so that he and others may refrain upon hearing that. He (PBUH) cursed the presser [of grapes to make wine] and the one who has it pressed, but many jurists permit one to press grapes for others even if he knew that he intended to make wine. This is a text outlines cursing the presser, with knowledge that judgment in excused defaulted for a deterrent.

He (PBUH) also cursed the maker and wearer of a wig, but some jurists only deem it disapproved.

He (PBUH) said, "Whosoever drinks in utensils of silver, in fact, kindles in his belly the fire of Hell," and some jurists deem it disapproved.

Similarly, his (PBUH) saying, "When two Muslims confront each other with their swords, both the murderer and the murdered are doomed to Hellfire" should be used as ground to forbid fighting believers unrightfully. However, we know that the people of the battles of the Camel and Siffin are not in Hellfire, because they have an excuse and a reasonable interpretation for fighting, as well as merits that prevented the requisite [result] from taking effect.

Removing Blame from Eminent Scholars

He (PBUH) said in the authentic hadith, "There are three persons whom Allah will neither talk to, look at, nor purify on the Day of Judgment, and they will have a painful punishment. [They are:] A man possessed superfluous water on a way and he withheld it from the travelers. Allah will say to him: "Today I withhold My Blessings from you as you withheld the superfluous part of that (water) which your hands did not create." A man who gives a pledge of allegiance to a Muslim ruler and gives it only for worldly gains. If the ruler gives him what he wants, he remains obedient to it, otherwise he does not abide by it. And a man bargains with another man after the `Asr prayer and the latter takes a false oath in the Name of Allah) claiming that he has been offered so much for the thing" This is a grave threat for the one who withholds his excess water, although a group of scholars permit man to withhold his excess water. This debate does not prevent us from believing in the unlawfulness of that based on the hadith, and the hadith does not prevent us from thinking that the interpreter is excused in that regard and will not be subjected to that threat.

He (PBUH) said, "Curse be upon Al-Muhallil (i.e. the one who marries a divorced woman with the intention of making her lawful for her former husband) and upon Al-Muhallal (i.e. the one for whom she is made lawful)" which is an authentic hadith that was narrated from him through multiple paths and was narrated from his Companions as well. Nevertheless, a group of scholars permitted Al-Muhallil's marriage in general, and some permitted it if it was not stipulated in the contract, and they have well-known excuses in this regard. For the Qiyas of foundations for the former yields that marriage is not nullified with stipulated conditions or with the ignorance of either payments.

The Qiyas of foundations for the latter is that lacking a linked condition in the contracts does not change the legality of the contract. This hadith did not reach whoever upheld this view. This is what is apparent, for their preceding books did not include it. If it had reached them, they would have mentioned it either to uphold it or confute it, and if it reached them and they interpreted it, believed in its abrogation or had something to oppose it, we know that these [scholars] will not be subjected to such threatening if they deemed it lawful while believing it was so from that perspective. This does not prevent us from knowing that deeming it lawful is a cause of that threat, even if it defaulted for some people for the lack of a reason or the existence of a deterrent.

Similarly, Mu'awiyah attributed paternity of Ziad, who was born on the bed of Al-Harith ibn Kildah, to his father, because Abu Sufian said he was of his offspring, although he (PBUH) said, "He who (falsely) attributes his fatherhood to anyone besides his real father, knowing that he is not his father, will be forbidden to enter Jannah" He (PBUH) also said, "Whoever attributes his fatherhood to someone other than his (real) father, and takes someone else as his master other than his (real) master without his permission, will incur the Curse of Allah, the angels and all the people, and Allah will accept from him neither repentance nor a ransom" which is an authentic hadith, and he ruled that the child [born out of wedlock] belongs to the one on whose bed it is born, which among the unanimously upheld provisions. We know that whoever attributes his fatherhood to someone other than the owner of the bed will fall under the Messenger's (PBUH) saying. However, no one who is beneath the Companions – let alone a Companion – may be specified and believed to be subject to that threat, because it is possible that the Messenger's (PBUH) ruling that the child belongs to the one on whose bed it is born did not reach them and that they believe the child belongs to whoever impregnated his mother, and they thought Abu Sufian is the impregnator of Sumayyah, Ziad's mother. This ruling may be unknown to many people, particularly before the spreading of the Sunnah, because this was the custom before Islam, or for other deterrents that prevent the threat from taking effect, such as good deeds that erase the sins and so on.

This is a vast topic, and it includes all things made unlawful by the Book or the Sunnah of some of the elites of the Ummah did not know the forbidding evidence and deemed the deed lawful, or had other evidence confuting them and believed them to be superior, with Ijtihad in examining both arguments according to their intellect and knowledge. Unlawfulness has effects, such as the commission of sin, vilification, punishment, being branded disobedient and so on, but they have conditions and deterrents. Unlawfulness may be confirmed, while its effects are not due to the absence of its conditions or the existence of a deterrent. Alternatively, unlawfulness may be nonexistent for that person while existent for others.

We reiterated it because people have two views in this issue:

The First – which is the view of the majority of early scholars and jurists: is that Allah's provision is unchanged, and whoever went against it with reasonable Ijtihad is mistaken but excused or rewarded. Based on that, the deed committed by the interpreter is unlawful, but the effects of unlawfulness do not apply to him, because of Allah's pardoning of him, for He does not charge a soul except with that within its capacity.

The Second: is that it is not unlawful for him, due to the forbidding evidence not reaching him, despite it being unlawful for others. Thus, the action of the person is not unlawful in itself.

Both views are close, and the debate is similar to the debates in general. This is what could be said about the hadiths of threats when subject to a debate. Scholars unanimously agree to use them as grounds for making unlawful the deed of the threat, whether it [the threat] is agreed or debated upon. They even need to cite them as evidence more often in the instances of debate. However, they disagreed on using them as grounds for confirming the threat if they were not of certain denotations as we mentioned.

If it was said: Why don't you say that the hadiths of threats do not address the instances of debate but the instances of agreement? For every deed the committer of which is cursed or threatened with wrath or punishment is unanimously regarded as an unlawful deed. This is in order for a Mujtahid not to be subjected to the threat if he did what he believed to be lawful, for it is worse for the believer than it is for the committer, as he [the believer] is the one who commanded him [the committer] to do it. Therefore, he is necessarily subjected to the threat of the curse or the wrath.

We say: There are multiple points to the answer:

First: The unlawfulness itself may or may not be confirmed in an instance of debate. If it is not confirmed through any instance of debate, it must not be considered to be unlawful unless it is unanimously deemed unlawful, for everything the unlawfulness of which is debated is lawful. This contradicts the consensus of the Ummah and is necessarily known to be false in the religion of Islam. If it was confirmed even in one interpretation, the Mujtahid who deems this unlawful deed to be lawful will either be subjected to the dispraise and punishment of whoever permitted the unlawful or not. If it is said: "He is subjected to it," or it is said: "He is not subjected to it", then the same goes for the unlawfulness unanimously affirmed in the hadiths of threats, as well as the threats affirmed in the instances of debate in the manner we explained. Rather the threat is stated for the committer, but the punishment for one who originally deems lawful the unlawful is greater than the punishment of one who commits it without believing it to be lawful. Therefore, if the unlawfulness could be confirmed in the instances of debate, and the permitting Mujtahid was not subject to punishment for such permittance as he was excused for it, then the committer would be more worthy of being exempt from that threat. And just as it is not necessary for the Mujtahid to be subjected to the effects of such unlawfulness, such as dispraise and punishment, it is also not necessary to fall under the effects of the threat, for a threat is not except a form of dispraise and punishment. If he could be subjected to that category in general, then the answer for some of its forms is the answer for all other forms. It does not make a difference whether the dispraise is much or little, or whether the punishment is grave or light, for the jeopardy of little dispraise and punishment in this regard is like the jeopardy of much, for the Mujtahid will not be subjected by neither little nor much thereof, but he is rather subjected to the opposite of that, of reward and recompense.

Second: Whether the legality of the deed is subject to agreement or disagreement is external to the deed and its attributes. They are additional matters according to the lack of knowledge that some scholars had. If the general text is meant to apply to specific cases, evidence must be provided to indicate specification, either coupled with the speech – according to those who do not permit the delay in clarification – or delayed until necessary according to the majority of scholars. There is no doubt that the addressed with that at the time of the Messenger (PBUH) were in need of knowing the legality of the matter. If what is intended through the general text concerning the cursing of the usurer, the Muhallil and so on, what is unanimously deemed unlawful, which cannot be known except after the Prophet's (PBUH) death and the Ummah speaking about all the members of that general expression, he would have deferred clarification of his words until the entire Ummah discusses all its members, which is not possible.

Third: The Ummah was addressed with that speech to know the unlawful and avoid it, to base their consensus upon it and to cite it as evidence in their disputes. If the intended meaning was just what they agreed upon, knowledge of the denotation would be contingent upon consensus, so it could not be cited as evidence before consensus is reached, so it could not be basis for consensus, for the basis for consensus must be precedent to it, and cannot be subsequent to it, because that would create an infinite loop. For the people of consensus would not be able to cite the hadith as evidence for a certain meaning until they are certain it is the intended one, and they could not be certain it is the intended one until they reach consensus. Therefore, deduction becomes contingent upon the consensus before it, and the consensus becomes contingent upon the deduction before it if the hadith was their evidence, so the thing becomes reliant on the thing reliant on it, so it is impossible to exist and cannot be used as evidence in debate, as it does not exist. This prevents the hadith from indicating the provision in the instances of agreement and disagreement, which necessitates that none of the texts containing threatening for a deed indicate the unlawfulness of that deed, which is certainly false.

Fourth: This necessitates that none of these hadiths could be cited as evidence until after the Ummah unanimously agree on its denotation. Then, the first generation of scholars could not cite them as evidence, nor can anyone who heard it from the Messenger's (PBUH) mouth, and whenever a man heard a hadith like that, found that many scholars have upheld it, and didn't know of any opposition to it, he must look around whether there is anyone across the earth who contradicts it, and he may not cite it as evidence in an issue of consensus except after complete research. Then, the Messenger's (PBUH) hadith would cease to be an argument merely by the contradiction of a single Mujtahid, so the view of that individual would nullify the Messenger's (PBUH) words and his agreement would affirm the Messenger's (PBUH) words. Moreover, if that individual was in error, his error would nullify the Messenger's (PBUH) words, and all this is necessarily false. For if it were said: "It should not be cited as evidence until after unanimous certainty," the denotation of texts would be contingent on consensus, which contradicts the Ummah's consensus. Then, texts would have no denotation, for only the consensus is regarded, and the text is impact-less.

If it was said: "It is cited as evidence unless a debate is known to exist," then the view of one of the Ummah would nullify the denotation of the text, which also contradicts the Ummah's consensus, and is necessarily known to be false within the religion of Islam.

Fifth: He either stipulates for the generality of the command the entire Ummah's belief in the unlawfulness, or he just regards the scholars' belief as sufficient. If it is the former, he may not use the threat hadiths as grounds for the unlawfulness until he knows that the entire Ummah – even those who grew up in distant deserts and those who recently embraced Islam – believe this deed to be unlawful. No Muslim, or even a sane person, says that, for it is impossible to be certain of this condition fulfilment.

If it was said: "The belief of all scholars is sufficient," the response is: you stipulated the consensus of scholars lest the threat includes a Mujtahid even if he was in error, but the same applies for someone of the general public who did not hear the unlawfulness evidence. The danger of the curse applying to the former is the same as the danger of the curse applying to the latter.

It does not provide a way out of this dilemma to say that the former is among the elites of the Ummah and the virtuous righteous people, while the latter is at the distant edges of the Ummah, for their distinction from that side does not prevent sharing in that judgment. Just as Allah (the Exalted) forgives the Mujtahid who errs, He forgives the ignorant if he errs and was unable to learn. Nevertheless, the damage that occurs when an ordinary person commits a forbidden deed without knowing its unlawfulness or being able to know it is much less than the damage incurred by an Imam making lawful what Allah made unlawful without knowing its unlawfulness or being able to know it. That is why it is said, "Beware the scholar's slip up, for when he slips up, a world slips up."

Ibn Abbas (may Allah be pleased with both of them) said, "Woe to the scholar from his followers." If the scholar is pardoned despite the graveness of the damage stemming from his doing, the other one is more worthy of being pardoned for the lightness of his damage. Yes, they have another distinction, which is that the former was diligent and reached this view with Ijtihad, and he has of the merits of spreading knowledge and reviving the Sunnah what submerges this damage. Allah has distinguished them from that perspective, so He rewarded the Mujtahid for his Ijtihad and rewarded the scholar for his knowledge a reward in which the ignorant did not share. They are joined in pardon and separated in reward. The punishment befalling whoever does not deserve it is impossible, whether he was great or base. So, that impossible must be excluded from the hadith in a manner that includes both types.

Sixth: The text of some of the threat hadiths are subject do debate, such as cursing Al-Muhallal . Some scholars say that he does not incur a sin at all, for he was not a party in the first marriage contract in order to incur the curse for believing in the obligation of honoring the legalization (i.e. that he must marry his former wife after she became lawful to him). Whoever believes that the marriage of the former (i.e. Al-Muhallil) is sound even if the condition is nullified and that she became lawful for the latter (i.e. Al-Muhallal), he has exempted the latter from sin. Even for Al-Muhallil, for he is cursed either for making her lawful [to her former husband], for believing in the obligation of upholding the condition coupled with the contract (i.e. that he must divorce her and let her remarry her former husband), or for both of them. If it is the first or the third, the purpose is fulfilled, and if it is the second, that belief is what incurs the curse whether legalization occurred or not. Then, what is mentioned in the hadith would not be the cause of the curse, and the cause of the curse would be unmentioned, which is false.

In addition, that person who believes in the obligation of upholding the condition, if he is ignorant, then no curse befalls him, and if he knows it is not compulsory, then it is impossible for him to believe in the obligation, unless he opposes the Messenger (PBUH) and is therefore a disbeliever. Then, the meaning of this hadith would return to cursing the disbelievers, and disbelief has no part in denying this particular provision exclusively, for this is like someone saying: "Allah cursed whoever disbelieved the Messenger (PBUH) in his ruling that the divorce condition in the marriage contract is nullified." Moreover, the statement of the hadith is general in text and in meaning, and it is a general subject. Such generalness cannot be interpreted in this scarce denotation, for it will be incorrectness and inarticulateness, like those who interpreted his (PBUH) saying, "Any woman who gets married without the consent of her guardian ..." to mean the emancipating bondmaid. The reason for its scarcity is that the ignorant Muslim is not included in the hadith, the Muslim who knows that it is not compulsory to uphold this condition will not stipulate it and believe it must be upheld, unless he is a disbeliever, and the disbeliever does not marry in the Muslims' way unless he is a hypocrite, and the occurrence of such marriage in such way is among the most scarce of the scarce. If someone said: "Such denotation almost never comes to the speaker's mind," he would be correct. We have stated many proofs in other places that this hadith means the one who deliberately makes the woman lawful for her ex-husband even if he did not stipulate it in the contract.

Similarly, the threats of cursing, Hellfire and so on were stated in topics that are debated. Such as the hadith narrated by Ibn Abbas (may Allah be pleased with both of them), that the Prophet (PBUH) said, "Allah cursed the women who visit graves and those who build mosques over them and put torches (there)" Al-Tirmidhi said, "A good hadith."

However, women's visit [to the graves] were deemed permitted by some scholars while others deemed it disapproved but not forbidden.

Also, the hadith narrated by Uqbah ibn Aamir that the Prophet (PBUH) said, "Allah cursed those who have intercourse with women in their anuses"

And the hadith narrated by Anas (may Allah be pleased with him) that the Prophet (PBUH) said, "The importer is blessed with provision and the hoarder is cursed"

We have already stated the hadith concerning the three persons whom Allah will neither talk to, look at, nor purify on the Day of Judgment, and they will have a painful punishment, who included the one who withheld his surplus of water.

He (PBUH) cursed the seller of wine, when some of the early Muslims did sell it.

It was authentically narrated from him through multiple paths that he said, "Allah will not look, on the Day of Resurrection at the person who drags his garment (behind him) out of conceit." He also said, "There are three (types of) people whom Allah will neither talk to, look at, nor purify on the Day of Judgment, and they will have a painful punishment. One who lets down his lower garments (below his ankles) out of arrogance, one who boasts of his favors done to another; and who sells his goods by taking a false oath" Although a group of jurists stated that dragging one's garments and lowering them below the ankles in arrogance is disapproved and not forbidden.

He also said, "Allah will not look, on the Day of Resurrection at the person who drags his garment (behind him) out of conceit" which is among the most authentic hadiths, but there is known debate concerning the wearing of wigs.

Moreover, he (PBUH) said, "Whosoever drinks in utensils of silver, in fact, kindles in his belly the fire of Hell" and some jurists do not deem it forbidden.

Seventh: What necessitates generality is established, and the aforementioned opposition is not valid for confuting it, for its utmost capacity is to say: "Using it in the instances of agreement and disagreement necessitates the inclusion of some who do not deserve cursing." The response is: If specification contradicts the rule, then expanding it contradicts the rule. Therefore, those who are excused with ignorance, Ijtihad or Taqlid are excluded from that generality, although the ruling includes all the unexcused just as it includes the instances of agreement, for that specification is lower, so it is more appropriate.

Eighth: If we interpret the text in this way, then the text includes the reason for cursing, and the effect would have defaulted for the excluded due to a deterrent. There is no doubt that the one who promised and threatened does not have to exclude those for whom the promise or the threat defaulted for a deterrent. Then, the statement would be on the path of correctness. However, if we make the curse for committing what is unanimously deemed unlawful, or if the cause for the curse is the belief that contradicts the consensus, the cause of the curse would be unstated in the hadith. Moreover, this generality is also in need for specification. So, if specification is required in both cases, upholding it in the first manner is more appropriate, due to following the path of correctness and freedom of ellipsis.

Ninth: What necessitates this is to deny the reaching of the curse to the excused, and we have already stated that the threat hadiths intend to clarify that this deed is a cause of that curse, so it means to say: This deed is a reason for cursing. If that is said, it does not necessitate the materialization of the effect for every person, but it necessitates establishing the cause, and if the establishing of the cause is not followed by the effect, the is no harm. We have previously affirmed that slander does not befall the Mujtahid, so much so that we even say, "The one who deems lawful the unlawful incurs a greater sin than the one who commits it," but the excused is excused.

If it was said: Then who would be punished? The committer of the unlawful is either someone who performed Ijtihad or Taqlid, and both of them are exempted from punishment.

We say: There are multiple points to the answer:

First: What is intended is to clarify that this deed entails punishment, whether someone did commit it or not. If we assume that no one commits it except one for whom the conditions of punishment are absent or a deterrent thereof arises, that does not deny that the deed is unlawful. Rather we know it is unlawful so that whoever knows of its unlawfulness avoids it, and it is Allah's mercy for whoever commits it to have an excuse for it. This is like the fact that the minor sins are forbidden, although they are expatiated by refraining from major sins. This is the case for all debated unlawful deeds; if they are found to be unlawful – even if those who committed it, whether out of Ijtihad or Taqlid, are excused – that does not prevent us from believing in their unlawfulness.

Second: Clarifying the ruling is a reason for removing the doubt that deters the materialization of the punishment. For the excuse that stems from belief is not meant to remain, but is desired to be removed as much as possible. Otherwise, it would not have been compulsory to spread knowledge, leaving people in their ignorance would have been better for them and refraining from clarifying the evidence for the debated issues would have been better than clarifying them.

Third: Clarifying the ruling and the threat is a motive for the refrainer to continue refraining. Otherwise, committing it would be prevalent.

Fourth: This excuse is not an excuse except when it is unavoidable. Otherwise, whenever a man could know the truth and he neglected it, he is not excused.

Fifth: There may be among the people those who commit it without sufficient Ijtihad or Taqlid to justify it. This type has the reason for the threat established and the deterrent nonexistent. Thus, he is subjected to the threat and it befalls him unless another deterrent arises, such as repentance, expatiating good deeds and so on. This is a source of confusion. One may believe that his Ijtihad or Taqlid permits him to do it, and he may be right sometimes and wrong other times. However, as long as he diligently pursues the truth and is not turned away from it by inclination, Allah does not charge a soul except with that within its capacity.

Tenth: Just as keeping these hadiths with their entailments necessitates including some Mujtahids within the threat, separating them from their entailments also necessitates including some Mujtahids within the threat. Since it is necessary in both cases, the hadith remains free from opposition, so it must be upheld.

To clarify that: Many scholars expressed that the committer of the debated action is cursed, including Abdullah ibn Umar (may Allah be pleased with both of them), for he was asked about whoever married a woman to make her lawful to her former husband, unbeknownst to the woman or her former husband, so he said, "This is adultery, and not marriage. Allah cursed Al-Muhallil and Al-Muhallal." This is narrated from him through multiple paths and from others as well, including Imam Ahmad ibn Hanbal, for he said, "If he wanted to make her lawful [for her former husband], then he is Muhallil, and he is cursed." Similar views are narrated from groups of Imams in many instances of debate, concerning Khamr, usury and so on. If the legal cursing and other threats stated only concerned the instances of agreement, then those scholars have cursed whoever did not deserve to be cursed, and they would therefore be worthy of the threat mentioned in a number of hadiths, such as his (PBUH) saying, "The cursing of a believer is tantamount to killing him" and his (PBUH) saying – narrated by Ibn Masoud (may Allah be pleased with him), "Defaming a Muslim is evildoing and fighting him is disbelief." Both stated by Al-Bukhari and Muslim.

Abu Al-Dardaa' conveyed that he heard the Messenger (PBUH) say, "Those who frequently resort to taunting and cursing (people) would neither be accepted as witnesses nor as intercessors on the Day of Resurrection" Abu Hurairah reported that the Messenger (PBUH) said, "It does not seem proper for a Siddiq that he should be an invoker of curse" Abdullah ibn Masoud narrated that the Messenger (PBUH) said, "A believer is not a defamer nor a curser nor coarse nor obscene" Stated by Al-Tirmidhi and he deemed it to be a good hadith. In another report, he said, "A man who curses something unrightfully will have that come back on him"

This threat stated for cursing – so much so that it was said that whoever cursed someone unrightfully will be the cursed one, and that cursing is evildoing, and it expels one from among the Siddiqs, intercessors and witnesses – addresses whoever cursed someone unrightfully, so if the committer of the debated deed was not included in the text, he would not be worthy of cursing, so his curser would be deserving of that threat, and those Mujtahids who believed that the debated issue as included in the hadith would be worthy of such threat. If the danger is confirmed in case of excluding or including the debated issue, it is known that there is no harm, and there is no problem in citing the hadith as evidence. If the danger is not confirmed in one of the two cases, then no danger is necessary at all. This is because if causality is confirmed, and it is known that their inclusion in case of existence necessitates their inclusion in the case of nonexistence, then what is confirmed is one of two matters:

Either the existence of the cause and effect, which is the inclusion of them all.

Or the lack of existence of the cause and effect, which is the exclusion of them all. For if the cause exists, the effect exists, and if the cause does not exist, the effect does not exist. This much is sufficient to nullify the question, but what we believe is that they are not included in both cases as affirmed. That is because inclusion in the threat is contingent upon the lack of excuse for the action, as for the legally excused, the threat does not befall them at all. The Mujtahid is excused and even rewarded, so the condition for inclusion is nonexistent in his case, and he is therefore not included in it whether he believed in the predominant interpretation of the hadith or contradicted it with a justifiable contradiction.

This is an indisputable obligation, from which there is no escape except in a single direction, **which is for the inquirer to say**: I accept that some of the Mujtahid scholars believe the debated text is included in the threat texts, and he threatens according to that debated text based on that belief, so he curses, for example, whoever committed that action. However, he is mistaken in this belief a mistake for which he is excused and rewarded, so he is not subjected to the threat of whoever cursed unrightfully, as that threat, in my belief, is intended for cursing what is unanimously deemed unlawful. Therefore, whoever curses a cursing what is unanimously deemed unlawful, he will be subjected to the aforementioned threatening for cursing. However, if the cursing is debated, it is not included in the threat hadiths, just as the deed the lawfulness of which is debated and the committer of which is cursed is not included in the threat hadiths. Just as I excluded the debated issue from the first threat,

I will exclude the debated issue from the second threat, and I believe that the threat hadiths on both sides do not address the debated issue, neither in the lawfulness of the deed nor in the lawfulness of cursing its committer whether or not I believe in the lawfulness of the deed. For in both cases, I do not permit cursing its committer, and I do not permit cursing whoever cursed its committer, and I do not believe that the committer or the curser are included in a threat hadith, and I do not reproach the curser like one who believes he is subjected to the threat. Rather, his cursing for the committer of the debated deed is, in my perspective, one of the issues of Ijtihad. I believe in his error in this regard just as I believed in the permitting person's error. For there are views in the debated issue:

One: Lawfulness of the deed

Two: Unlawfulness of the deed and the materialization of the threat.

Three: Unlawfulness of the deed without the materialization of that grave threat.

I choose this third view, due to the establishment of evidence for the unlawfulness of the deed and the unlawfulness of cursing the committer of a debated deed. I also believe that the hadith stated in threatening the committer and threatening the curser did not include these two cases.

The inquirer is told: If you accepted the cursing of the committer to be an issue of Ijtihad, it is permitted to prove it with the predominant interpretation of texts, because then there is no avoidance from the debated issue being intended by the threat hadith, and the evidence for intending it is established, so it must be upheld. Alternatively, if you did not accept it to be an issue of Ijtihad, cursing him would be certainly forbidden. There is no doubt that whoever cursed a Mujtahid a certainly forbidden cursing is subjected to the threat stipulated for the curser, even if he had an interpretation, such as someone who cursed some of the early righteous Muslims. Thus, it is confirmed that causality is compulsory whether you are certain of the unlawfulness of cursing the committer of the debated deed or if you permitted the debate therein. That belief you mentioned does not confute citing the threat texts as evidence in both cases, which is clear.

He is also told: Our aim here is not to discuss whether the threat addresses the debated issue, our aim is to discuss citing the threat hadith as evidence in the debated issue. The hadith yielded two rulings: unlawfulness and threat. What you mentioned only addresses confuting its proving of the threat only, but the intended point here is to clarify its proving of the unlawfulness. If you maintain that the hadiths threatening the curser do not mean debated cursing, there would be no evidence for forbidding the debated cursing, and as for what we have of the debated cursing as previously mentioned, if it is not forbidden, it is permitted.

Or he is told: If there is no evidence for its unlawfulness, its unlawfulness must not be believed when the evidence for its permissiveness is established, namely the hadiths cursing whoever did that. Scholars, may Allah be merciful to them, debated the lawfulness of cursing him, and there is no evidence for the unlawfulness of forbidding cursing him with that interpretation. Thus, the evidence for permitting cursing him which is free from opposition must be upheld. This nullifies the question, for the matter has been deflected to the inquirer from another angle. That deflection came because the majority of the texts forbidding cursing include threat, so if the threat texts cannot be cited as evidence in a debated issue, they cannot be cited as evidence for debated cursing, as previously mentioned.

If he said: I cite consensus as evidence for forbidding this cursing.

He is told: Consensus is established for forbidding cursing certain persons of the people of virtue. As for cursing a qualifier, you know it is debated, and we have previously mentioned that cursing the qualifier does not necessitate befalling every one of its members, unless the conditions are met and the deterrents are absent, and this is not the case.

He is also told: All the evidence already mentioned against interpreting these hadiths in the issue of consensus come here, and they nullify the question here, just as they nullified the origin of the question. This is not of the sense of making the evidence an introduction to another evidence so that it may be said: "This – with elaborateness – is one evidence," for the aim is to clarify that the danger they presumed is necessary in both cases, so it is not a problem. Therefore, a single evidence will have indicated intending the debated issue with the texts, and that there is no problem therein. It is not uncommon for the evidence for an issue to be an introduction to the evidence for another issue, regardless of the two issues being correlative.

Eleventh: Scholars agree that the threat hadiths must be upheld concerning the unlawfulness they indicate, but some of them disagreed about upholding individual hadiths thereof regarding the threat in particular. As for the unlawfulness, there is no considerable debate. Scholars, of the Companions, Followers and jurists after them all kept citing them as evidence in the debated issues and elsewhere. Rather if the hadith contained threat, it is stronger in conveying unlawfulness than what the hearts know. We have also already outlined the superiority of the view of those who uphold it concerning the provision and the threat, and that it is the majority's view.

Therefore, a question that contradicts the consensus is not accepted.

Twelfth: The threat texts in the Book and the Sunnah are very abundant, and upholding their entailment is compulsory generally and absolutely, without naming a specific person and saying that this person is cursed, that he incurred the wrath [of Allah] or that he deserves Hellfire, particularly if that person has virtues and good deeds, for everyone except Prophets are susceptible to sins, minor and major, while it is possible for that person to be a Siddiq, a martyr or a pious person, due to what is previously mentioned that the effect of the sin is avoided with repentance, invocation of forgiveness, erasing good deeds, expatiating calamities, accepted intercession or merely for the will and mercy of his Lord.

So, if we uphold the entailment of His (the Almighty) saying, "Indeed, those who devour the property of orphans unjustly are only consuming into their bellies fire. And they will be burned in a Blaze." [4:10].

His (the Almighty) saying, "And whoever disobeys Allah and His Messenger and transgresses His limits - He will put him into the Fire to abide eternally therein, and he will have a humiliating punishment." [4:14].

His (the Almighty) saying, "O you who have believed, do not consume one another's wealth unjustly but only [in lawful] business by mutual consent. And do not kill yourselves [or one another]. Indeed, Allah is to you ever Merciful. And whoever does that in aggression and injustice - then We will drive him into a Fire. And that, for Allah, is [always] easy." [4:29-30], and so on of the threat verses.

Or if we uphold His (PBUH) saying, "Allah curses whoever drinks wine, whoever is ungrateful to his parents, or whoever changes land boundary markers."

Or, "Allah cursed the thief"

Or, "Allah cursed the accepter of usury its payer, the two witnesses and one who records it"

Or, "Allah cursed the withholder of alms and the transgressor therein"

Or, "He who made any innovation in Madinah or gave refuge to an innovator, there is upon him the curse of Allah, that of the angels and that of all the people"

Or, "Allah will not look, on the Day of Resurrection at the person who drags his garment (behind him) out of conceit"

Or, "He who has, in his heart, an ant's weight of arrogance will not enter Paradise"

Or, "He who cheats us is not one of us"

Or, "Whoever attributes his fatherhood to someone other than his (real) father, and takes someone else as his master other than his (real) master without his permission, Paradise is forbidden for him"

Or, "Whoever acquires the property of a Muslim by taking a false oath, will meet Allah Who will be angry with him"

Or, "The one who severs the ties of kinship will not enter Paradise"

And so on of the threat hadiths, we are not allowed to specify someone who committed one of these deeds and say: "This specific person is subjected to that threat," due to the possibility of repentance and other punishment-expungers. We may not say either: "This necessitates cursing the Muslims, cursing the Ummah of Muhammad (PBUH) or cursing the Siddiq and the righteous." For it is said: When the righteous Siddiq commits one of these deeds, there must be a deterrent that prevents the effect of the threat from reaching him with the establishment of its cause. Thus, committing these deeds by someone who believes they are permitted through Ijtihad, Taqlid and so on, its end is for him to be a type of Siddiqs whom the threat did not reach because of a deterrent, such as those whom the threat did not reach due to a repentance, expatiating sins and so on.

Be aware that this is the path that must be treaded, for there is nothing else except two wretched roads:

The First: is believing that the threat reaches every individual and claiming that this is the result of upholding the texts. This is uglier than the views of the Kharijites who regard the committers of sins as infidels, the Mutazilites and so on, its corruption is necessarily known, and its evidence is known in instances other than this one.

The Second: Disregarding the hadiths of the Messenger (PBUH) thinking that upholding them necessitates slandering those who contradict them. Such disregard leads to aberration and following in the footsteps of the people of the two books who, "have taken their scholars and monks as lords besides Allah, and [also] the Messiah, the son of Mary" [9:31]. For the Prophet (PBUH) said, "hey did not worship them, but when they made something lawful for them, they considered it lawful, and when they made something unlawful for them, they considered it unlawful." It also leads to obeying the creature in Allah's disobedience, and it leads to ill consequence and poor result understood from the denotation of His (the Almighty) saying, "O you who have believed, obey Allah and obey the Messenger and those in authority among you. And if you disagree over anything, refer it to Allah and the Messenger, if you should believe in Allah and the Last Day. That is the best [way] and best in result" [4:59].

Moreover, the scholars, may Allah be merciful to them, disagree a lot, so if every reproach-containing report contradicted by someone had its reproach disregarded or was disregarded entirely, damage too great to be described will be incurred, of disbelief and apostasy, and if the damage of this was not greater than the damage of the previous one, it would certainly not be less than it.

Therefore, we must believe in the Book entirely, follow what was revealed to us from our Lord–all of it, not to believe in part of the Scripture and disbelieve in part, and not to have our hearts incline to follow some parts of the Sunnah and have an aversion to other parts based on habits and inclinations, for this is departure from the straight path to the path of those who have evoked Allah's anger or of those who are astray.

May Allah (the Almighty) guide us to what He loves and accepts of words and deeds in goodness and wellbeing for us and all Muslims. Amen. All praise is due to Allah, Lord of the worlds, and may Allah bestow His mercy and abundant peace upon our Master Muhammad–the final Prophet, his good and pure family, his chosen Companions, his wives-the mothers of believers, and those who follow them with good conduct until the Day of Judgment.

The End

www.ingramcontent.com/pod-product-compliance
Lightning Source LLC
Chambersburg PA
CBHW031125160426
43192CB00008B/1116